THE SURVEY KIT

Purpose: The purposes of this 9-volume Kit are to enable readers to prepare and conduct surveys and become better users of survey results. Surveys are conducted to collect information by asking questions of people on the telephone, face-to-face, and by mail. The questions can be about attitudes, beliefs, and behavior as well as socioeconomic and health status. To do a good survey also means knowing how to ask questions, design the survey (research) project, sample respondents, collect reliable and valid information, and analyze and report the results. You also need to know how to plan and budget for your survey.

Users: The Kit is for students in undergraduate and graduate classes in the social and health sciences and for individuals in the public and private sectors who are responsible for conducting and using surveys. Its primary goal is to enable users to prepare surveys and collect data that are accurate and useful for primarily practical purposes. Sometimes, these practical purposes overlap the objectives of scientific research, and so survey researchers will also find the Kit useful.

Format of the Kit: All books in the series contain instructional objectives, exercises and answers, examples of surveys in use and illustrations of survey questions, guidelines for action, checklists of do's and don'ts, and annotated references.

Volumes in The Survey Kit:

1. **The Survey Handbook**
   Arlene Fink

2. **How to Ask Survey Questions**
   Arlene Fink

3. **How to Conduct Self-Administered and Mail Surveys**
   Linda B. Bourque and *Eve P. Fielder*

4. **How to Conduct Interviews by Telephone and in Person**
   James H. Frey and *Sabine Mertens Oishi*

5. **How to Design Surveys**
   Arlene Fink

6. **How to Sample in Surveys**
   Arlene Fink

7. **How to Measure Survey Reliability and Validity**
   Mark S. Litwin

8. **How to Analyze Survey Data**
   Arlene Fink

9. **How to Report on Surveys**
   Arlene Fink

THE SURVEY KIT 2

HOW TO ASK
SURVEY
QUESTIONS

ARLENE FINK

SAGE Publications
International Educational and Professional Publisher
Thousand Oaks   London   New Delhi

10/99

32552393

For information address:

SAGE Publications, Inc.
2455 Teller Road
Thousand Oaks, California 91320
E-mail: order@sagepub.com

SAGE Publications Ltd.
6 Bonhill Street
London EC2A 4PU
United Kingdom

SAGE Publications India Pvt. Ltd.
M-32 Market
Greater Kailash I
New Delhi 110 048 India

Printed in the United States of America

Library of Congress Cataloging-in-Publication Data

Main entry under title:

The survey kit.
    p. cm.
    Includes bibliographical references.
    Contents: v. 1. The survey handbook / Arlene Fink — v. 2. How to ask survey questions / Arlene Fink — v. 3. How to conduct self-administered and mail surveys / Linda B. Bourque, Eve P. Fielder — v. 4. How to conduct interviews by telephone and in person / James H. Frey, Sabine Mertens Oishi — v. 5. How to design surveys / Arlene Fink — v. 6. How to sample in surveys / Arlene Fink — v. 7. How to measure survey reliability and validity / Mark S. Litwin — v. 8. How to analyze survey data / Arlene Fink — v. 9. How to report on surveys / Arlene Fink.
    ISBN 0-8039-7388-8 (pbk. : The survey kit : alk. paper)
    1. Social surveys. 2. Health surveys. I. Fink, Arlene.
HN29.S724   1995
300'.723—dc20   95-12712

This book is printed on acid-free paper.

                    99 10 9 8 7

Sage Production Editor: Diane S. Foster
Sage Copy Editor: Joyce Kuhn
Sage Typesetter: Janelle LeMaster

Contents

How to Ask Survey Questions:
Learning Objectives

The aim of this book is to guide the reader in preparing and using reliable and valid survey questions. The following specific objectives are stated in terms of aspirations for the reader.

- Understand a survey's cultural, psychological, economic, and political context by:

  - Identifying specific purposes

  - Preparing appropriately worded, meaningful questions for participants

  - Clarifying research and other objectives

  - Determining a feasible number of questions

  - Standardizing the questioner

  - Standardizing the response choices

- Ask valid questions that:

  - Make sense to the respondent

  - Are concrete

  - Use time periods that are related to the importance of the question

  - Use conventional language

  - Use short and long questions appropriately

  - Use loaded words cautiously

- Avoid biasing words
- Avoid two-edgers
- Avoid negative phrasing
- Compare the characteristics and uses of closed and open questions
- Distinguish among response formats that use nominal, ordinal, and numerical measurement
- Identify correctly prepared questions

- Correctly ask questions by:

  - Using response categories that are meaningfully grouped
  - Choosing an appropriate type of response option
  - Balancing all responses on a scale
  - Selecting neutral categories appropriately
  - Determining how many points to include on a rating scale
  - Deciding where to place the positive or negative end of the scale
  - Determining the proper use of skip patterns

- Apply special questioning techniques to survey knowledge, attitudes, and demographics

1 Asking Questions: A Matter of Context

A survey is a system for collecting information to describe, compare, or explain knowledge, attitudes, and practices or behavior. Surveys are taken of political and consumer choices, use of health services, numbers of people in the labor force, and opinions on just about everything from aardvarks to zyzyvas.

Individuals, communities, schools, businesses, and researchers use surveys to find out about people by asking questions about feelings, motivations, plans, beliefs, and personal backgrounds. The questions are typically arranged into mailed or self-administered questionnaires and into in-person (face-to-face) or telephone interviews. Because **questions** are the focus of many surveys, learning how to ask them in written and spoken form is essential.

The way you ask survey questions prescribes the answers, as you can see from Example 1.1.

EXAMPLE 1.1
The Relationship Between
Questions, People, and Information

Three survey experts were invited to present the results of their survey "American Views on Taxation." Expert A's presentation was entitled "Most Americans Support Increased Taxes for Worthy Purposes." Expert B's speech was called "Some Americans Support Increased Taxes for Worthy Purposes." Expert C's talk was named "Few Americans Support Increased Taxes for Worthy Purposes." A review of the talks and original surveys revealed three questions:

Expert A's: Would you support increased taxes to pay for education programs for very poor children?

Expert B's: Would you support an increase in your taxes to pay for education programs for very poor children?

Expert C's: Would you support a 10% increase in your taxes to pay for education programs for very poor children?

As you can see, three surveyors with competing agendas can come up with entirely different questions, responses, and interpretations.

Surveys are used as a source of information in research and evaluation studies and in planning programs and setting policy in health, education, business, and government. This book focuses on guidelines for asking questions for all these survey uses.

The selection and wording of questions are strongly influenced by the survey's context: its purposes, who asks the questions, how they are asked, who answers them, and the characteristics of respondents and responses. Consider the two surveys in Example 1.2.

EXAMPLE 1.2
Survey Questions and Their Context

Survey 1

Lancaster, a community of about 150,000 people, is planning programs to prevent child abuse and family violence. The community intends to conduct a survey in which families are asked to identify their problems and to suggest solutions to them. The results will be used to guide the development of programs to prevent and treat alcohol use, social isolation, and unemployment. These problems and others like them are known to be prevalent in the community. Research has linked them to abuse and violence.

Parents with school-age children in 4 of the city's 10 school districts will be mailed a survey questionnaire to complete in the privacy of their homes. The survey, which focuses on educational needs, takes 20 minutes to complete and is written in the five languages most commonly spoken in the community. All responses are anonymous. Respondents are given statements and asked to rate on a scale from 1 to 4 whether they strongly agree, agree, disagree, or strongly disagree with each. The questionnaire has been endorsed by prominent members of the community and the city.

Survey 2

The Children's Clinic is a school-based clinic in a very low-income area of a large city. The clinic intends to conduct a survey in which families and teachers are asked to identify children's health problems (including medical and psychosocial issues) that the clinic might address. A sample of parents, teachers, health professionals, and children will be interviewed in person. The interview will take 30 minutes and will be conducted in English and Spanish. About half the questions will use ratings and rankings; the remainder will allow respondents to give answers in their own words. All responses will be confidential. A report of the results will be available in 12 months.

The two surveys described in Example 1.2 are different in several ways. These differences influence the choice, characteristics, and number of questions, as shown in Example 1.3.

EXAMPLE 1.3
Two Surveys

	Survey 1: A Mailed Questionnaire Concerning Child Abuse	Survey 2: Interviews About the Services of a School-Based Clinic	Effect on Questions
Purpose	Identify needs and solutions to guide program development	Identify needs to guide focus of clinic services	Survey 1: Questions are about education Survey 2: Questions are about health
Respondents	Parents of school-age children	Parents, teachers, health professionals, and children	Survey 1: Questions posed are for parents only Survey 2: Questions posed are for people of differing roles and ages
Surveyor	Self-administered, mailed questionnaire contains the questions	Interviewers ask face-to-face questions	Survey 1: Questions must be easily read and understood without outside assistance Survey 2: Questions must be worded so that they can be understood orally

	Survey 1: A Mailed Questionnaire Concerning Child Abuse	Survey 2: Interviews About the Services of a School-Based Clinic	Effect on Questions
Responses	Closed: Ratings are made on a scale from 1 to 4	Some questions use ratings and rankings; the remainder rely on the respondent's own words	Survey 1: Responses can be translated on a scale from 1 to 4 Survey 2: Half the responses will come from ratings and rankings; the remainder will be in participants' own words
Timing	Survey takes 20 minutes	Survey takes 30 minutes	Survey 1: Respondents may not return questionnaires, or they many not answer all questions Survey 2: Time must be allocated for reading and interpreting respondents' answers
Resources	Need translation into five languages Survey must be printed and mailed	Need translation into English and Spanish Interviewers must be hired and trained	Survey 1: Expertise is needed in five languages Survey 2: Expertise is needed in two languages
Privacy	All responses will be anonymous	All responses will be confidential (codes will replace names)	Survey 1: "Sensitive" questions (e.g., about drug use and sexual habits) are more likely to be answered Survey 2: Must be a little more "careful" with sensitive questions as respondents can be traced

The two surveys described in Examples 1.2 and 1.3 aim to guide the development of programs and the focus of services to prevent child abuse and family violence and to promote health. The first survey is for parents only; the second is for parents, teachers, health professionals, and children. Because the first survey is self-administered, the questions must be worked on until they are understandable by respondents without assistance from the survey team. The results of the second survey will require the surveyors to have special expertise in interpretation and classification of the responses that are given in the participants' own words. The first survey will need resources for printing and mailing; the second will need funding for hiring and training interviewers. Because the first survey is anonymous, the surveyors may be able to ask questions about topics that named respondents might be reluctant to discuss. Confidential answers remove some of the anonymity and so may reduce the respondents' frankness. The first survey needs to be translated into five languages; the second survey is to be given in English and Spanish.

A survey's purpose, surveyors, and respondents (along with other considerations) must be fully understood before you begin to write questions. The following is a checklist to use in identifying and understanding a survey's context.

Checklist for Deciding the Survey's Context

✓ **Identify the survey's specific purposes.**

The purpose of a survey is its hoped-for outcomes. Usually, you have a general purpose in mind, say, to find out about job satisfaction, preferences for certain products, or voting plans. If you are concerned with job satisfaction, for example, the survey should focus on that topic. Questions about previous jobs, hobbies, personal background, and so on may not be relevant.

✓ Clarify the terms used to state the survey's purpose.

In Example 1.2, the first survey's questions focus on educational needs. This term is very general. Educational needs may include completing high school and obtaining vocational training as well as acquiring specific skills like how to be a parent, to cook, and to manage money.

The second survey in Example 1.2 is about the health needs of children. Definitions of health are far from uniform and vary according to culture. To select appropriate and usable definitions for a survey, you can review what is known and published about a topic. You can also define the term yourself. The problem with creating your own definition is that others may not be convinced of its validity. Sometimes, it is best to adopt a respected definition and even, if possible, an already tested set of questions.

Choices regarding the focus and definitions used in survey questions are sometimes made when you know its specific objectives.

✓ Be sure to have the specific objectives of the survey in place.

The specific objectives refer to the precise information the survey is to collect. Sometimes, the objectives take the form of research hypotheses or questions. At other times, the objectives are written as statements. Consider these sample objectives for Survey 1 (Example 1.2):

1. Identify the most common needs for educational services

2. Determine the extent to which differences exist among the needs of parents of differing ethnicities/races

3. Determine the extent to which differences exist in needs between men and women

4. Identify if parents are willing to participate in job retraining programs

5. Find out if parents are satisfied with their current educational status

A specific set of objectives like these suggests a survey that asks questions about the following:

- Educational needs (Objective 1)
- Ethnicity/race (Objective 2)
- Gender (Objective 3)
- Willingness of respondents to participate in job retraining (Objective 4)
- Satisfaction with current educational status (Objective 5)

Suppose another surveyor added these objectives:

6. Compare younger and older parents in their needs to learn how to manage a household and care for a child

7. Determine the relationship between parents' education and method of disciplining children for mild, moderate, and severe infractions

To collect information for the new objectives, Survey 1 would need to add questions on the following:

- Age of parents
- How parents manage their household
- How parents care for their children

- Level of parents' education
- Methods for disciplining children for mild, moderate, and severe infractions

Before preparing a survey, all potentially imprecise or ambiguous terms used in the survey's specific questions have to be clarified or defined. For the questions above, the imprecise terms are: needs; educational services; ethnicity/race; willingness; satisfaction; younger and older; effective household management; effective child care; discipline; and mild, moderate, and severe infractions. Why are these terms ambiguous? No standard definition exists for any of them. What are needs, for example, and of the very long list that you might create, which will be included on the survey? What is effective child care? What is discipline? How do you distinguish satisfied from dissatisfied parents?

EXERCISE

The following are four sample specific objectives for Survey 2 (Example 1.2):

1. Find out where children usually receive their health care
2. Identify barriers to using preventive health services, such as vaccinations
3. Identify if differences exist in the health care needs of younger and older children of differing ethnicities/races.
4. Compare the health status of boys and girls of differing ethnicities/races

   □ Add at least three more objectives
   □ Describe the data that the survey must collect to meet all seven objectives (the first four above and the three you have added)

☐ List all terms that will need to be defined or clarified before good questions can be written

■ **SUGGESTED ANSWERS** ■

Two additional objectives:

5. Compare the barriers to use of health services among older and younger parents whose children will use the clinic
6. Determine if respondents are satisfied with the quality of the health services their children currently receive

Data to be collected:

- Barriers to the use of health services
- Age
- Ethnicity/race
- Health status
- Satisfaction with quality of health services

Definitions and clarifications needed:

- Health services
- Barriers
- Younger and older
- Ethnicity/race
- Health status
- Satisfaction

✓ Know the respondents.

Questions should be written so that they encompass your needs for data, but they must also be formulated so that respondents can answer them easily and accurately. Check the appropriateness of the language level. Reading abilities may vary considerably even for the same survey. For example, a survey of parents in a school district may include some people who read extremely well and others who read poorly. If so, you will have to decide how to state the questions to maximize the number of respondents who can read and comprehend all questions.

Make sure that respondents have sufficient knowledge to answer the questions. Facing unanswerable questions is extremely frustrating for the respondent. In a survey to find out about the quality of education, many people may not be able to answer a question like the following:

What role should the Department of Curriculum and Instruction play in setting educational standards for this community?

Unless told, many people might not know about the department's current authority, how it is administered, and how it has been designed to fit into the community. They may not have a clue about the department's role. In their frustration, they may guess or they may refuse to answer the question or any other question on the survey.

Survey respondents may also have difficulty answering questions that ask them about past or future actions and behaviors. For example, if you ask relatively healthy survey respondents about their health exactly 1 year ago on this date, they may have forgotten because they have no compelling reason to dwell on their health. Also, if you ask people to tell you who they will elect to the Board of Education in 6 months, they may not yet know. Asking respondents to compare their behavior to that of others sometimes results in confusion. Asking employees to compare the adequacy of child care at your company to that provided by other firms, for example, is likely to produce poor results unless you are certain that your employees are familiar with the child-care practices of other companies.

✓ **Carefully match what you need to know against the time you have to find out.**

The number of questions to include in a survey depends largely on the amount of time available for the survey. A half-hour interview is usually able to include more questions than a 10-minute interview. The number of questions in a survey also depends on what you need to know and how many questions are needed for adequate measurement.

Suppose that in Example 1.2, Survey 1, the survey of parents is allotted 20 minutes. Suppose also that it is supposed to cover 10 topics: educational needs; ethnicity/race; gender; willingness of respondents to participate in job retraining; satisfaction with current educational status; age of parents; how parents manage their household; how parents can care for their children; level of parents' education; and methods for disciplining children for mild, moderate, and severe infractions. The surveyor can ask one or more questions to cover each topic or ask 10 questions about any single topic. To decide on which questions to ask, you must balance what you need to know (the specific objectives), the number of questions needed to cover each topic covered by the objective, and the amount of time available for the survey.

A good way to get started in determining the number of questions for each topic is to make a chart like the one shown in Example 1.4.

EXAMPLE 1.4
Topics, Number of Questions, and Information Collected

Topic	Number of Questions	Information Collected
Educational level	1	Last year of school completed
Educational needs	10	Whether had training for specific jobs (e.g., sales, nurses aide, etc.)
Ethnicity/race	1	African American, White but not Latino, Latino/Latina, Chinese, Southeast Asian, Other
Gender	1	Male/Female
Satisfaction with current educational status	1	Yes, no
Willingness to participate in job retraining	1	If needed: yes, no, do not know, or not sure
Age	1	Whether under 18 years of age, between 18 and 20, between 21 and 30, and over 30
Managing a household	6	Manage financial affairs (e.g., balance checkbook, shop for food for a week, monitor household repairs)
Caring for the child	5	Doctor's visits, supervise school work, know names of friends
Discipline methods	8	Methods (e.g., talking, hitting, yelling) for mild (e.g., not answering a question), moderate (e.g., coming home more than an hour late), and severe (e.g., not coming home at all) infractions
Total	35	

Remember that Survey 1 (Example 1.2) is to last 20 minutes. To find out if the 35 questions can be answered in the 20 minutes available, the survey must be tried out in advance of use with potential respondents or people just like them. To determine if the questions adequately cover the topics, you can ask experts, search other surveys, and conduct statistical analyses to find out if parents who are known to cope well answer the questions differently from parents who are known to cope poorly.

✓ Standardize the surveyor.

The ideal standardized surveyor asks questions the same way every time. When two surveyors who are conducting the same survey are indistinguishable from one another in their delivery and findings, they are standardized.

Standardized surveyors can take human form, as in face-to-face or telephone interviews, or they can take the form of a self-administered questionnaire. A self-administered questionnaire can be mailed to respondents or completed in a specially designated area such as a clinic waiting room, a classroom, or a personnel office. Example 1.5 illustrates the use of standardized surveyors.

EXAMPLE 1.5
Standardized Surveyors

1. A survey of parents is conducted to find out if they are willing to participate in a program to prevent child abuse and neglect. A 25-item questionnaire is mailed to 200 parents. The questionnaire was tried out with 50 parents before it was considered

suitable. The original version had 35 questions, but that was considered by parents to take too much time to answer. Questions were omitted if 10 or more parents either would not or could not complete them. All questions are accompanied by four choices, and the respondent is to circle the one "best" answer.

2. Interviews were conducted to compare the views of managers and sales staff regarding a program to introduce more flexible hours for employees. The Human Resources Department trained five of its staff to conduct the interviews. The training took 6 hours, and quality checks of a sample of interviews were made to ensure that each interviewer followed very strict question-asking guidelines.

✓ **Standardize the response format.**

A standardized format asks each respondent to select from a list of preset choices. Example 1.6 distinguishes between standardized formats and other types.

EXAMPLE 1.6
Standardized and Other Response Formats

Standardized Format

Directions: To what extent do you agree with the following statements about the purpose of pretesting self-administered survey questionnaires? In a pretest, a draft of the survey is tried out with a sample of people, and their reviews are incorporated into the final version. *Circle one choice for each statement.*

Purpose of Pretesting?	Strongly Agree (1)	Agree (2)	Disagree (3)	Strongly Disagree (4)	No Opinion (5)
To find out if the questions are appropriate for the respondents	1	2	3	4	5
To determine if any questions are misleading	1	2	3	4	5
To examine whether surveyors can appropriately use the survey forms	1	2	3	4	5
To determine if the information obtained by the survey is reliable	1	2	3	4	5
To determine if the information obtained by the survey is valid	1	2	3	4	5

Not Standardized

Directions: Explain the extent of your agreement with the following statement:

"Self-administered questionnaires should be tried out in advance of their use to see if they provide consistent and accurate data. An advance trial means testing the logistics of the survey (the ease with which the interviewers can record responses) as well as the survey form itself."

Write your explanation here:

Some people may have difficulty with standardized question-and-response formats. They may object to the structure or be unfamiliar with it. When this happens, the surveyor should try to find another standardized format that is acceptable to the respondents or look for an alternative way of getting the information. One way that is currently in use is to tape the questionnaire. This seems to have the effect of making the structure more palatable.

✓ **Remember that questions are asked in a social, cultural, and economic context.**

In the two survey situations illustrated in Example 1.2, the survey instruments are to be translated from English into another language. To ensure that you are asking questions that are meaningful to people speaking that language, rely on survey experts and potential respondents to help with the wording of the questions. Remember also to budget time and money for these activities.

Another contextual factor to consider is whether the answers will be anonymous. If so, you may be posing different kinds of questions than you would otherwise. Surveyors agree generally that more "sensitive" questions can be asked about personal behaviors and beliefs in anonymous surveys (where the identity of the respondent is not known) than can be asked in confidential surveys or in those in which the respondent's name is common knowledge.

Guidelines for
Asking Survey Questions

The following are guidelines for asking survey questions. You may find that in your survey some guidelines are more important than others.

ASK PURPOSEFUL QUESTIONS

Purposeful questions are those that are logically related to the survey's objectives. In a survey about airline travel, respondents will expect questions about the food, service, on-time record, and so on. If questions are asked that do not seem to be about airline travel (they are about age or reading habits, for instance), explain the reason for them: "Some of our questions are about your background and preferences so that we can examine whether Uniting Airlines is meeting the needs of all its passengers."

ASK CONCRETE QUESTIONS

A concrete question is precise and unambiguous. Questions are precise and ambiguous when, without prompting, two or more potential respondents agree on the words used in the question. For example, suppose you want to find out about people's perceptions of their health and you ask them to describe it. A person who is generally well but has been sick this past week might answer differently from another individual who was desperately ill all year but is now feeling better. To help make a question more concrete, add a time period:

Less concrete: How would you describe your health?

More concrete: In the past 3 months, how would you describe your health?

The more detail you can provide, the more reliable the answer is likely to be. For example, in providing a time period, avoid asking about usual or typical behavior. Instead, provide a specific time period, as illustrated in Example 1.7.

EXAMPLE 1.7
Using Specific Time Periods
to Make Questions More Concrete

Poor: How often do you exercise in a typical week?

Better: How often did you exercise during the past week? (Start with today's date and count back 7 days.)

Detailed questions alway help produce reliable answers. For example, if you are surveying responses to a play, rather than just asking a general question about enjoyment of the play, decide on the components of the play that are the most important to the survey, as in these examples.

Less concrete: Did you enjoy the play?

More concrete: Did you enjoy the first act of the play?

Even more concrete: Did you find the comedy scenes in the play's first act funny?

EXERCISE

Make these three questions more concrete and describe how you improved specificity.

1. How satisfactory was your stay at the hotel?
2. What is the best way to improve health care?
3. Which restaurants do you eat in most frequently?

■ POSSIBLE ANSWERS ■

1. How satisfactory was room service during your stay at the hotel?

   The question has been made more specific by focusing on room service.

2. What is the best way to improve the quality of preventive health care?

   "Improve" has been clarified to concentrate on the quality of preventive care.

3. In the past 3 months, which New York restaurants did you eat in most frequently?

   A time period and a place have been set: in the past 3 months and New York, respectively.

USE TIME PERIODS THAT ARE RELATED
TO THE IMPORTANCE OF THE QUESTION

Periods of a year or more can be used for major life events like the purchase of a house, occurrence of serious illness, birth of a child, or death of a parent. Periods of a month or less should be used for questions that are less important. Asking people to remember relatively unimportant events over long periods of time leads to too much guessing. You do not want the period to be too short either because the event in question may not have occurred during the interval. Example 1.8 illustrates good and poor use of time periods in survey questions.

EXAMPLE 1.8
Use of Time Periods in Survey Questions

Poor: How long did it usually take for you to fall asleep during the past 6 months?

Comment: Too much time has probably elapsed for the respondent to recall accurately. Also, the amount of time to fall asleep may have varied considerably, making estimation a truly difficulty task.

Better: How long did it usually take for you to fall asleep during the past 2 weeks?

Poor: In reference to your car accident of a year ago, how many visits have you made to a physician in the past 6 weeks?

Comment: The number of visits made to the doctor in the past 6 weeks is probably different from the number made in the first weeks after the accident.

Better: In reference to your car accident of a year ago, look at the following list and tell how many visits you have made to a physician.

USE CONVENTIONAL LANGUAGE

A survey is not a conversation. To get accurate information, survey questions rely on standard grammar, punctuation, and spelling. You should use words that maximize understanding for everyone in the survey. This is often difficult to do. All questions should be reviewed and tested by people who are proficient in reading and speaking the language in which the survey is written, content experts, and potential respondents.

Guidelines for Using Conventional Language When Asking Survey Questions

The following are guidelines for using conventional language in surveys.

USE COMPLETE SENTENCES

Complete sentences, whether as statements or questions, express a clear and complete thought, as illustrated in Example 1.9.

EXAMPLE 1.9
Using Complete Sentences and Questions

Poor: Place of residence?

Comment: Place of residence means different things to different people. For example, I might answer Los Angeles, but another respondent might say California, the United States, or 15 Pine Road.

Better: What is the name of the city where you currently live?

Poor: Accidents among children are . . .

Comment: This statement is unclear. A respondent might say "terrible," "the leading cause of death among children under the age of 12 years," "underreported," "a public health problem," and so on.

Better: Indicate the extent of your agreement with the statement "Accidents among children are a public health problem in the United States."

AVOID ABBREVIATIONS

You should avoid abbreviations unless you are certain that they are commonly understood. Most people probably are familiar with USA and FBI; many would be familiar with the abbreviations for their cities, states, provinces, universities, and so on. But don't count on it. If in doubt, spell it out, as shown in Example 1.10.

EXAMPLE 1.10
Avoiding Abbreviations

Poor: In your view, does USC provide a liberal arts education worth its yearly tuition?

Comment: If this question is being asked of many Californians, USC will stand for the University of Southern California. But for others, USC can mean University of South Carolina or University of Southern Connecticut.

Better: In your view, does the University of South Charleston provide a liberal arts education worth its yearly tuition?

AVOID SLANG AND COLLOQUIAL EXPRESSIONS

Slang and colloquialisms should be avoided because they go out of fashion quickly and not everybody keeps up with the newest expressions. Some exceptions exist. You may want to use slang for a survey of a homogeneous group who share a special language, such as workers in the same job or profession, people with similar health or social problems, and teenagers.

The problem in using slang and colloquialisms is that if you plan to report the results of the survey to a general audience, you need to translate the slang. Less than expert translation may result in loss of meaning.

BE CAREFUL OF JARGON
AND TECHNICAL EXPRESSIONS

Survey questions should avoid jargon and technical terms (see Example 1.11). If you have reason to believe that your group is homogeneous and familiar with the terms, you can use them. However, you must then be concerned with how understandable a wider audience will find the results.

EXAMPLE 1.11
Avoiding Jargon and Technical Terms

Poor: Should a summative evaluation of Head Start be commissioned by the U.S. government?

Comment: The term "summative evaluation" is used among some specialists in program evaluation. It means a review of the activities and accomplishments of a completed program or of one that has been in existence for a long time.

Better: Should the U.S. government commission a history of Head Start to review its activities and accomplishments?

HAVE THE QUESTIONS REVIEWED BY EXPERTS

Experts are individuals who are knowledgeable about survey question-writing or the subject matter addressed by a survey. Experts can tell you which survey questions appear too complex to be administered easily and too long or too difficult to be answered accurately.

HAVE THE QUESTIONS REVIEWED
BY POTENTIAL RESPONDENTS

Potential respondents are people who are eligible for the survey. Eligible people are the population or sample that you want to hear from. For example, if you plan to survey teens in high school to find out about their eating habits, then the reviewers should be high school teenagers. A review by potential respondents helps guarantee that the survey's questions are meaningful and inclusive of all important ideas.

ADOPT OR ADAPT QUESTIONS THAT HAVE
BEEN USED SUCCESSFULLY IN OTHER SURVEYS

A great many survey questions are available to the public. Among these are questions asked by the U.S. Census. Questions like these have already been reviewed and used and shown to collect accurate information. Use them for your survey, when appropriate.

USE SHORTER QUESTIONS WHEN YOU
NEED TO SAVE TIME, MINIMIZE READING,
OR ARE SATISFIED WITH BRIEF ANSWERS

Shorter questions save time and require relatively little reading. They also tend to provide less detailed information. Longer questions often provide background information to respondents and help them recall or think about why they did something or hold a particular view.

> *Short:* Have you ever traveled to another country? If yes, how important was the scenery in your decision to take a trip?
>
> *Long:* Travel to other countries has become increasingly popular in this country. Have you ever traveled to another country? If yes, you might have traveled to other countries to enjoy their scenery. How important was the scenery in deciding to take a trip?

Long questions are useful in getting information on sensitive concerns (e.g., health and sexual habits) and socially controversial issues (e.g., gun control and substance abuse). When using longer questions in self-administered questionnaires, consider the time they take to ask or read and answer. Example 1.12 shows the use of a longer question.

EXAMPLE 1.12
Longer Questions

"A diagnosis of prostate cancer can have a profound effect on the quality of life of older men and their families. At least three treatments are available to men with prostate cancer: observation, surgery, and radiation. Your husband (partner) has chosen surgery. How much influence did you have in your husband's (partner's) choice of treatment?"

USE LOADED QUESTIONS, IF NECESSARY, BUT BE CAUTIOUS

Surveyors sometimes deliberately load a question to get information on embarrassing or controversial topics. The purpose of the loading is to encourage respondents to give a "true" response rather than just one that is socially acceptable. Two kinds of loading are often used, as illustrated in Example 1.13.

EXAMPLE 1.13
Loaded Questions Used in
Prompting the Respondent

1. *You are not alone.* Parents get really angry at their children sometimes. In the past week, have you been really angry at your son?

2. *You are in the best company.* Many prominent people have publicly admitted that they have sought help for problems related to alcohol abuse. In the past year, have you been to see a physician or other health professional because you thought you were drinking too much?

Use loaded questions with caution. People may see through them, get annoyed, and either not answer the question or answer it inaccurately.

AVOID BIASING WORDS AND PHRASES

Biasing words and phrases elicit emotional responses that may have little to do with the issues addressed by the survey. They are considered biasing because they trigger an emotional response or a prejudice. Some words and expressions like this are abortion, pro-life, creationism, secular humanism, and people's right to bear arms.

The bias in words tends to change with time. "Socialist" and "communist" now rarely evoke much emotional response in the United States, although they did so for 50 years. Other words and phrases simply die out, are discarded, or replaced. Drug addict, for example, has been replaced by substance abuser (or user).

Bias may arise if the surveyor does not fully understand the culture and values of the respondents and asks questions that are inadvertently offensive. To guard against this possibility, all questions must be reviewed and pilot tested before they are used.

AVOID TWO-EDGED QUESTIONS

A two-edged question contains two ideas. An example is "Do you think we should continue to use tax money to support arts and sports programs in the public schools?" This question is really twofold: "Do you think we should continue to use tax money to support art programs?" and "Do you think we should continue to use tax money to support sports programs?" Certainly, some people would support the arts programs, some the sports, others both, and still others neither. No matter what the respondent answers, however, you will not know what he or she means. To avoid asking two-edged questions, check the use of the word "and" in the question.

AVOID NEGATIVE QUESTIONS

Negative questions are difficult for many respondents to answer because they require an exercise in logical thinking. For example, suppose a question asked respondents if they agreed or disagreed with the statement "The United Nations should not have more authority to intervene in a nation's military affairs." Some respondents will fail to read the word "not." Others will first translate the negative into the positive and ask "Do I think the United Nations should have more authority to intervene in a nation's military affairs?" If you do use a negative, be sure to emphasize the negative word: "The United Nations should **NOT** have more authority to intervene in military affairs."

2 Keep Questions Closed or Open Them Up?

Questions take one of two primary forms. When they require respondents to use their own words, they are called open. When they are preselected for the respondent, they are called closed. In general, closed questions are considered more efficient and reliable than open questions for getting information from groups of people. Both types have advantages and limitations.

Open Questions

An open question allows respondents to give answers in their own way. These questions are useful in getting unanticipated answers and for describing the world as the respondent really sees it rather than how the researcher does. Some respondents also prefer to state their views in their own words. Sometimes, the responses provide quotable material. The responses to open questions, however, are often difficult to compare and interpret. Consider the question in Example 2.1.

EXAMPLE 2.1
Open Question and Three Answers

Question: How often during the past month did you find yourself having difficulty trying to calm down?

Answer 1: Not often

Answer 2: About 10% of the time

Answer 3: Much less often than the month before

Open questions provide answers that must be catalogued and interpreted. Does 10% of the time (Answer 2) mean not often (Answer 1)? How does Answer 3 compare to the other two? Open questions are used primarily in making decisions about individuals rather than groups. Experts in qualitative research are experienced in cataloguing and interpreting open questions.

Closed Questions

Closed questions are more difficult to write than open ones because the answers or response choices must be known in advance. However, some respondents prefer closed questions because they are either unwilling or unable to express themselves while being surveyed. Finally, closed questions produce standardized data that can be analyzed statistically. Statistical analysis is essential in making sense of survey data for groups of people (e.g., teams, schools, teens, the elderly, Americans). Also, because the respondent's expectations are more clearly spelled out, the answers have a better chance of being more reliable or consistent over time. Closed questions are easy to standardize. Example 2.2 shows a closed question.

EXAMPLE 2.2
Closed Question

How often during the past month did you find yourself having difficulty trying to calm down?

(Circle **one** number)

Always	1
Very often	2
Fairly often	3
Sometimes	4
Almost never	5
Never	6

How do you decide when to use open and closed questions? The following checklist can be used in choosing which type to ask.

Checklist for Deciding Between
Open and Closed Questions

	✓ If yes, use OPEN	✓ If yes, use CLOSED
Purpose	Respondents' own words are essential (to please respondent, to obtain quotes, to obtain testimony)	You want data that are rated or ranked (on a scale of very poor to very good, for example) and you have a good idea of how to order the ratings in advance
Respondents' characteristics	Respondents are capable of providing answers in their own words Respondents are willing to provide answers in their own words	You want respondents to answer using a prespecified set of response choices
Asking the question	You prefer to ask only the open question because the choices are unknown	You prefer that respondents answer in their own words
Analyzing the results	You have the skills to analyze respondents' comments even though answers may vary considerably You can handle responses that appear infrequently	You prefer to count the number of choices
Reporting the results	You will provide individual or grouped verbal responses	You will report statistical data

3 Responses: Choices and Measurement

W hen respondents give answers in their own words, the questions are open. When the spectrum of possible answers is provided to the respondent, the question is closed. Open questions consist of the question alone. Closed questions consist of the question and the response choices.

Response Choices

The choices given to respondents for their answers may take several forms. One form is called nominal or categorical. (The two terms are often used interchangeably.) Categorical choices have no numerical or preferential values. For example, asking respondents if they are male or female calls for categorical choices: Two categories are named—male and female. The second type of response choice is called ordinal. Respondents who are asked to rate or order choices (say, from very positive to very negative) are given ordinal choices. Numerical response choices call for numbers, such as age or height.

Categorical, ordinal, and numerical response choices are illustrated in Example 3.1.

EXAMPLE 3.1
Three Common Response Choices

1. **Categorical (or nominal):** *Name* or *categorize* your astrological sign. Check *one* only.

[ ] Aquarius	[ ] Leo
[ ] Pisces	[ ] Virgo
[ ] Aries	[ ] Libra
[ ] Taurus	[ ] Scorpio
[ ] Gemini	[ ] Sagittarius
[ ] Cancer	[ ] Capricorn

2. **Ordinal:** Tell into which of the following age groups, *given in order from youngest to oldest*, you fit best. Circle *yes* or *no* for each.

Years of Age	Yes (1)	No (2)
Under 25	1	2
25 - 30	1	2
31 - 40	1	2
41 - 55	1	2
56 - 65	1	2
Over 65	1	2

3. **Numerical:** As of your most recent birthday, *what number of years tells* how old you are?

_____ years old

The first question asks for the name or category of astrological signs and implicitly provides information on the month in which each respondent was born. A survey result might be "At least 34% of respondents are Aries, who were born between March and April." The second question is different in the information it provides because it results in a hierarchy. A sample result might be "At least 50% of the sample is under 50, but only 5% is over 65 years of age." The third question uses a number to determine age. A survey result might be "The average age is 26 years."

Which format should you use? To decide, you must first know what each can do for your survey.

Consider the three questions in the next example, Example 3.2. These questions have been designed for a survey whose main purpose is to guide curriculum development in colleges. As in Example 3.1, the three types of response choices are represented: categorical, ordinal, and numerical.

Suppose the objectives of the survey in Example 3.2 are these:

- Identify books and plays that are considered important reading for graduates.
- Examine the relationship between the books and plays people read and those they rate as being important.
- Examine the relationship between respondents' age and the books and plays they rate most and least important.

EXAMPLE 3.2
Three Questions
About Important Literature

1. **Nominal or categorical:** Which of these books or plays have you read? Circle yes *or* no for each choice.

Have you read each of these?	Yes (1)	No (2)
Oedipus Rex	1	2
Pride and Prejudice	1	2
The Vicar of Wakefield	1	2
Bible	1	2
Moby Dick	1	2
The Glass Menagerie	1	2

2. **Ordinal:** How important to a college graduate's education is each of the following books and plays? Use the following scale to make your rating:

$$1 = \text{Definitely unimportant}$$
$$2 = \text{Probably unimportant}$$
$$3 = \text{Probably important}$$
$$4 = \text{Definitely important}$$
$$5 = \text{No opinion/Don't know}$$

Books/Plays	Circle ONE for each literary work				
Oedipus Rex	1	2	3	4	5
Pride and Prejudice	1	2	3	4	5
The Vicar of Wakefield	1	2	3	4	5
Bible	1	2	3	4	5
Moby Dick	1	2	3	4	5
The Glass Menagerie	1	2	3	4	5

3. **Numerical:** What is your date of birth?

_____ _____ 19 _____

Month   Day   Year

Each of the questions in Example 3.2 produces a different kind of information. The first question asks respondents to tell if they have read each of six works of literature. The second question asks the respondent to use a continuum to indicate how important each of the six works is. This continuum has been divided into four points (with a "no opinion/don't know" option). The third question asks respondents to specify the month, day, and year of their birth.

Survey questions typically require three basic tasks of respondents, use three "scales," and produce three measurement patterns or types of data. The three questions in Examples 3.1 and 3.2 represent the three tasks, scales, and data.

The first question in Example 3.2 asks respondents to tell whether or not they fit into one of two categories: read this book or did not read this book. Data or measures like these have no natural numerical values and are called **categorical** or **nominal.** A hypothetical survey finding that uses categorical data might take this form: "Over 75% of the respondents read at least one book or play on the list, but no one read all six. Of 75 respondents, 46 (61.3%) indicated they had read the *Bible,* the most frequently read book."

Categorical measures result in counts and frequencies expressed as numbers and percentages.

The second measurement pattern, represented by the second question in Example 3.2, is called **ordinal.** A response is made to fit on a continuum or scale that is ordered from positive (very important) to negative (very unimportant). The information from scales like this is called ordinal because an ordered set of answers results. Ordinal data consist of the numbers and percentages of people who select each point on the scale. In some cases, you may find it expedient to compute the average response: the average rating of importance across all respondents. Sample survey results might take a form like this: "Of 75 respondents completing this question, 43 (57.3%) rated each book or play as definitely or probably important. The average ratings ranged from 3.7 for the *Bible* to 2.0 for *The Vicar of Wakefield.*"

Surveys often ask respondents for **numerical** data. In Example 3.2, respondents are asked for their birth date. From the date, you can calculate each respondent's age. Age is considered a numerical and continuous measure, starting with zero and ending with the age of the oldest person in the survey. When you have numerical data, you can perform many statistical operations. Typical survey findings might appear as follows: "The average age of the respondents was 43 years. The oldest person was 79 years, and the youngest was 23. We found no relation between age and ratings of importance."

CATEGORICAL OR NOMINAL MEASURES: HOW TO GET THEM

The first question in Example 3.2 asks respondents to answer yes or no regarding whether they read a named book or play. "Yes" and "no" are categories into which the responses must be placed. Other commonly used response categories are "present" or "absent" and "applies" or "does not apply." If you ask 100 respondents the name of the country of their birth, and 20 answer France and 80 say the United States, you have categorical data that can be described this way:

	Yes	No
Born in France?	20	80
Born in the United States?	80	20

When you ask people the name of their country of birth, astrological sign, ethnicity, and so on, you are collecting categorical data. In this case, it is also called nominal because the name determines the category.

Questions about gender and race/ethnicity produce nominal or categorical information, as shown in Example 3.3.

EXAMPLE 3.3
Nominal or Categorical Data From Surveys

1. Indicate your gender by circling the appropriate number.

	Yes (1)	No (2)
Female	1	2
Male	1	2

2. Which best describes your race/ethnicity? Circle *one* choice only.

Race/Ethnicity	Yes (1)	No (2)
White, not Latino	1	2
Latino	1	2
African American	1	2
Native American	1	2
Asian		
(please specify_____)	1	2

Other examples of nominal or categorical measures are questions like these:

- Which of the following medical problems do you have? Hypertension; diabetes; low back pain.

- Are you currently married? Living with someone but not married? Not currently married and not living with someone? Married but living alone?

- Do you have a BA? MA? MEd? MSW? PhD? MD?

CATEGORICAL RESPONSES AND WHO'S ELIGIBLE

Nominal or categorical responses put respondents into categories such as male or female, Native American or African American. Questions asking respondents to categorize or name themselves are used to get demographic information and help decide who should be included (or excluded) from a survey. Suppose you are planning to ask people to rate the importance of six books or plays. To get accurate information, you want to survey people who know what they are doing. You might decide to exclude potential respondents who have read only four or fewer. A question asking for categorical answers would then be appropriate:

- Which of the following books have you read? Check all that apply.

      _____ *Pride and Prejudice*
      _____ *The Vicar of Wakefield*
      _____ *Bible*
      _____ *Moby Dick*
      _____ *Madame Bovary*

The responses to "check all that apply" questions are almost always categorical. The reason is that each check means "Yes, I belong in the category." Each category or choice that is left blank is assumed to mean "No, I do not belong."

CATEGORICAL RESPONSES ARE EXCLUSIVE

Categorical response choices should be mutually exclusive. Compare the following good and poor questions and response categories.

Poor: Which of the following best describes you?

	Yes (1)	No (2)
Professional	1	2
Registered nurse	1	2
Nurse practitioner	1	2
Administrator	1	2
Nurse midwife	1	2

Comment: The categories for the responses are not mutually exclusive. The choice "professional" can include all of the remaining categories. A nurse practitioner, a registered nurse, a nurse midwife, and an administrator can be considered professionals. To confuse matters even more, the nurse practitioner, administrator, and nurse midwife may all be registered nurses.

Better: Which of the following apply to you? Answer yes *or* no for each category.

	Yes (1)	No (2)
Nurse practitioner	1	2
Administrator	1	2
Registered nurse	1	2
Nurse midwife	1	2

CATEGORICAL RESPONSES ARE INCLUSIVE

Categorical response categories should be inclusive and exhaustive. Include all categories on which you hope to get information. The following are illustrations of two questions that might be asked in a survey of lawyers to identify how many of them had specific expertise in various kinds of legal problems.

Poor: Which **one** of the following best describes your primary expertise?

[ ] Landlord-tenant problems
[ ] Consumer problems
[ ] Traffic cases
[ ] Other (specify) _____

Comment: These categories are not exhaustive. The survey is likely to produce more responses in the "other" category than in the three that are listed.

Better: Which **one** of the following best describes your primary expertise?

[ ] Landlord-tenant problems
[ ] Consumer problems
[ ] Traffic cases
[ ] Small claims
[ ] Misdemeanors
[ ] Felony cases
[ ] Wills
[ ] Personal injury claims
[ ] Domestic relations
[ ] Adoption
[ ] Tax
[ ] Real estate
[ ] Bankruptcy
[ ] Poverty
[ ] Other (specify) _____

CATEGORICAL RESPONSES AND MEANING

A major issue in asking questions that produce categorical responses is how to group responses so that they are meaningful. A general rule is to use groups that make sense in the survey and that also will be useful when you report the results of the survey. Suppose you were conducting a survey of elderly people and you wanted to know how many in your survey fell into certain categories or age groups. You could frame your question as in Example 3.4.

EXAMPLE 3.4
Question for Older People

Which best describes your age group? Circle **one** choice only.

Age Group	Yes (1)	No (2)
65 - 74	1	2
75 - 84	1	2
85 - 95	1	2
Over 95	1	2

The question and responses used above are fairly standard. If you look at surveys of older persons, you will find that the response groups used in the question are typical. One good way to be sure you are using meaningful categories is to adapt or adopt those used in other surveys. Already existing and in-use choices tend to make reporting easier because they are familiar.

Existing response choices may not always suffice to meet the needs of a particular survey; then, of course, you must create your own. Question 2 in Example 3.3 used standard racial/ethnic terms to describe categories for a survey of prenatal care and low income in Northern California. At the time of the survey (1992), these groupings accounted for 98% of women who were likely to be in any survey of prenatal care in the geographic region. Terms change over time, and so the ones in the question may seem out of place or time just a few years later. Be cautious in using questions from other surveys and standard terms for job descriptions, names of countries, and income groups. These terms change.

Example 3.5 shows two questions about age that might be used in a study of music listening.

EXAMPLE 3.5
Choosing Response Choices

1. We conducted a survey to compare teens and others in their music-listening habits. We asked this question:

Which best describes your age? Circle **one.**

Years of Age	Yes (1)	No (2)
12 or younger	1	2
13 - 14	1	2
15 - 17	1	2
18 - 21	1	2
22 - 30	1	2
31 or older	1	2

2. We conducted a survey to compare the music-listening habits of people of differing ages. We asked the following question:

Which best describes your age? Circle **one.**

Years of Age	Yes (1)	No (2)
20 or younger	1	2
21 - 30	1	2
31 - 40	1	2
41 - 50	1	2
51 - 60	1	2
61 or older	1	2

The purpose of Question 1 is to produce information for comparing teens and nonteens. All people 31 or older are grouped together.

The aim of Question 2 is to obtain data for comparing people of differing ages. The groupings assume that

1. Music-listening habits vary according to age decade (e.g., 31-40 and 51-60), and

2. All people under 20 years of age have similar listening habits and all those 61 and older have similar listening habits OR

3. The differences in music-listening habits between people under 20 and between those 61 and older are not important for the survey's purposes.

Questions With Ordered Responses: How to Get Ordinal Data Using Common Rating Scales

Questions that ask respondents to order their responses are ordinal measures. Question 2 in Example 3.2 is a typical ordinal measure. In the question, respondents are asked to create an order by rating importance on a scale from 1 to 4. In so doing, they are making an implicit statement about the relative importance of one literary work ("definitely important") over another ("definitely not important.") When responses are ordered or placed in ordered groupings along one dimension, you have ordinal data. The most familiar kinds of ordinal data come from scales like the following:

- Strongly agree, agree, neither agree nor disagree, disagree, strongly disagree
- Excellent, very good, good, fair, poor
- Always, very often, fairly often, sometimes, almost never, never

■ Completely satisfied, very satisfied, somewhat satisfied, somewhat dissatisfied, very dissatisfied, completely dissatisfied

Ordinal measures are extremely common in surveys. In fact, typical surveys tend to have more ordinal measures than any other kind. When asking questions that require respondents to order their answers, you need to be concerned with the content of the choices, the number of choices, whether to include a middle point and a "do not know" response, and a range of grammatical and other issues including how the question looks on a page or sounds when spoken in person or on the telephone. Tune in on a conversation between two surveyors about ordered responses:

Surveyor A: I am conducting a survey of anxiety and depression in the workplace. I'd like to ask "In the past month, how often has feeling depressed interfered with doing your job?" What response choices can I use so that I can compare the number of people who feel depressed most often with the number of people who feel depressed least often?

Surveyor B: You need a set of response choices that are ordered on a scale ranging from "often" to "not often."

A: What scales are available?

B: You have several options. You can use a simple 3-point scale with response choices like "often," "sometimes," "never"; a 4-point scale like "nearly all the time," "some of the time," "a little of the time," "almost none of the time"; a 6-point scale like "all of the time," "most of the time," "a good bit of the time," "some of the time," "little of the time," "none of the time." You can also create longer scales if you want. I can even think of situations in which discrete numerical categories might be appropriate. These categories could be "100% of the time," "between 50% and 100% of the time," and "less than 50% of the time."

A: How do I make my decision?

B: Before I answer, I want to raise some issues to consider in asking respondents to order their responses, such as whether to include a middle point ("neither agree nor disagree," for example) and whether to include a "don't know" or "no opinion" choice.

A: Do you know of some guidelines for me to use in asking this type of question and determining response choices?

B: You're in luck. I just came across a set.

Guidelines for Asking Closed Questions and Determining Ordered Responses or Scales

USE A MEANINGFUL SCALE

A meaningful scale is one that makes sense in terms of the survey's specific objectives. In the preceding conversation, Surveyor A wants to compare people in terms of the frequency of their depression. Surveyor B has suggested a number of response choices. To choose among them, Surveyor A can do any or all of the following:

- Ask potential respondents which scale is best.
- Ask other surveyors to help select a scale.
- Try one or more scales on a preliminary basis and select the one that gives a good "spread" of answers (you do not want everyone to choose just one point on the scale) and is meaningful to the respondent.

CONSIDER FIVE TYPES OF RESPONSE OPTIONS

Endorsement: Definitely true, true, don't know, false, definitely false

Frequency: Always, very often, fairly often, sometimes, almost never, never

Intensity: None, very mild, mild, moderate, severe

Influence: Big problem, moderate problem, small problem, very small problem, no problem

Comparison: Much more than others, somewhat more than others, about the same as others, somewhat less than others, much less than others

---

EXERCISE

Surveyor A wants to study the frequency with which depression interferes with job performance. Suppose the surveyor asks you for a question that results in comparative information. Write the question.

■ ANSWER ■

Compared to your usual performance on the job, how has your depression affected your performance in the past 4 weeks?

Please circle ONE response

Much worse than usual	1
Somewhat worse than usual	2
About the same as usual	3
Somewhat better than usual	4
Much better than usual	5

BALANCE ALL RESPONSES

A scale is balanced when the two endpoints mean the opposite of one another and the intervals between the points on the scale are about equal. "Much worse" (see the preceding exercise) is the opposite of "much better," and the meaning of the interval between "much worse" and "somewhat worse" is similar in degree to that of "somewhat better" and "much better." "About the same as usual" appears to fit in the middle. Of course, language is imprecise, and the intervals may be less equal than they appear on the face of it. That's why all questions should be tried out before they are used. Examples of how to balance scales follow:

#1 *Poor:*

- Yes, constantly
- Yes, very often
- Yes, once
- No, never

Better:

- Yes, constantly
- Yes, very often
- Yes, fairly often
- Yes, a couple of times
- Yes, once
- No, never

#2 *Poor:*

- Very happy
- Somewhat happy
- Neither happy nor unhappy
- Not very happy

Better:

- Very happy
- Happy
- Somewhat happy
- Neither happy nor unhappy
- Somewhat unhappy
- Unhappy
- Very unhappy

USE A NEUTRAL RESPONSE
CATEGORY ONLY IF IT IS VALID

Provide a neutral category only when you are sure it is a valid response. A neutral category is either a middle point (neither happy nor unhappy) or "no opinion," "don't know." Some surveyors believe that neutral choices provide respondents with an excuse for not answering the question. If not answering is a possibility, pretest the question with and without the neutral choices and compare the results. How many responses cluster around the middle point? Do some respondents resent not having a middle point? As part of the pretesting process, ask the respondents about the scale. Did they encounter any problems in using it? Would another set of responses be more appropriate?

USE 5- TO 7-POINT RATING SCALES

Current thinking suggests that 5- to 7-point scales are adequate for the majority of surveys that use ordered responses. Self-administered questionnaires and telephone interviews should probably use 4 or 5. In-person interviews should use visual aids for scales with 5 or more points on them, such as the following sample:

MUCH WORSE THAN USUAL	1
SOMEWHAT WORSE THAN USUAL	2
ABOUT THE SAME AS USUAL	3
SOMEWHAT BETTER THAN USUAL	4
MUCH BETTER THAN USUAL	5

Conclusive evidence supporting odd or even scales is unavailable. Use odd or even depending on the survey's needs.

PUT THE NEGATIVE END
OF THE SCALE FIRST

Consider putting the negative end of the scale first for questions that are potentially embarrassing or about socially undesirable behaviors or attitudes, as illustrated in Example 3.6.

EXAMPLE 3.6
Putting the Negative End of the Scale
First When Questions May Be Embarrassing

How much do these statements apply to you? Circle **one** number for each line.

Embarrassing Statement	Very Much (4)	Much (3)	A Fair Amount (2)	A Little (1)	Not at All (0)
I find that my clothes do not fit.	4	3	2	1	0
I am uncomfortable with the changes in my body.	4	3	2	1	0
I frequently feel anxious.	4	3	2	1	0

In this question, the negative end of the scale means agreeing that the statement applies "very much." If you put the positive end first (that is, the statement applies "not at all"), people may just select that as the least embarrassing option. Deciding which end of the scale to place first is most important in face-to-face interviews and least important in anonymous self-administered and other mail surveys. If the survey deals with a problem the respondent thinks is important, the direction of the scale may not count at all. If the questions above, for example, are asked of cancer patients, you do not have to worry as much about directionality as you do if the questions are meant for teens.

KEEP QUESTIONNAIRES UNCLUTTERED
AND EASY TO COMPLETE

Present the question in an uncluttered, easy-to-complete way in self-administered questionnaires (including mail questionnaires). This can be achieved by following the rules in Example 3.7.

EXAMPLE 3.7
Rules for Presenting
an Uncluttered Question

1. Tell the respondent how and where to mark the responses.

Emphasize any special tasks or requirements in the question, as shown below:

Example

Considering your reading habits, **during the past year** how often did you read the following newspapers, journals, and magazines? Circle **one** for each choice.

Periodical	Never (1)	Rarely (2)	Sometimes (3)	Frequently (4)	Always (5)
New York Times	1	2	3	4	5
Wall Street Journal	1	2	3	4	5
Cosmopolitan	1	2	3	4	5
New England Journal of Medicine	1	2	3	4	5
Sports Illustrated	1	2	3	4	5

2. *Avoid questions with skip patterns in self-administered questionnaires.*

A skip pattern is a question that you expect does not apply to all participants. If you must use skip patterns, set them off as clearly as possible, as shown below:

Example

14. Have you had **two years or more in your life** when you felt depressed or sad most days, even if you felt OK sometimes?

    [ ] No → **GO TO QUESTION 15**
    [ ] Yes ____
          ↓

        14A. Have you felt depressed or sad much of the time in the **past year?**

            [ ] Yes
            [ ] No

3. *Organize responses so that they are readable.* Consider the following:

Poor: To what extent do you agree or disagree with the following statements?

    1. Each day of work feels as if it will never end.

____ Strongly agree ____ Undecided ____ Agree ____ Disagree ____ Strongly disagree

2. Most of the time I have to force myself to go to work.

[ ] Strongly agree   [ ] Undecided
[ ] Agree   [ ] Disagree
[ ] Strongly disagree

Item 1 is poor because the lines before the choices sometimes appear as if they are after the choices. For example, the line that precedes "agree" is also right next to "strongly agree." Item 2 is poor because the choices are not aligned, and the logic of the scale disappears.

Better:

	Strongly Agree (1)	Agree (2)	Undecided (3)	Disagree (4)	Strongly Disagree (5)
Each day of work feels as if it will never end.	1	2	3	4	5
Most of the time I have to force myself to go to work.	1	2	3	4	5

QUESTIONS SHOULD BE WRITTEN SO THAT INTERVIEWERS CAN DISTINGUISH BETWEEN WORDS READ TO RESPONDENTS AND WORDS THAT ARE INSTRUCTIONS/OPTIONS (Example 3.8).

EXAMPLE 3.8
Distinguishing Between Words for Respondents, Instructions, and Options

Which of the following have you (or SOMEONE IN YOUR FAM-ILY) done in the last year with a neighbor? HAND RESPONDENT CARD A. CODE YES OR NO FOR EACH ITEM ANSWERED.

	Yes (1)	No (2)
Stopped and talked when we met	1	2
Had dinner together at their home or ours	1	2
Had dinner together at a restaurant	1	2
Watched their home when on vacation, or they watched ours	1	2

In this example, the use of capitalized bold letters tells the interviewer to give the respondent an option: (or SOMEONE IN YOUR FAMILY). The question for respondents is in regular letters, and the instructions are capitalized. Notice that the interviewer is asked to present Card A to the respondent. Face-to-face or in-person interviewers use cards that contain the scale and its definition when respondents are asked to select from among five or more choices. Telephone interviewers read the choices before asking the question and repeat them for each question.

**USE RANKINGS ONLY IF RESPONDENTS
CAN SEE OR EASILY REMEMBER ALL CHOICES.**

Rankings or rank-order scales are a type of ordinal measure in which choices are placed in order from the highest to the lowest (or the other way around). The rank of students in a college senior class is important to graduate school admissions committees, for example. The following is typical of questions asking respondents to rank their preferences:

■ Select the **three** most important books or plays for reading by U.S. college graduates from the following list.

Oedipus Rex
Pride and Prejudice
The Vicar of Wakefield
Bible
Moby Dick
The Glass Menagerie
Other (specify) _____

   Put your choices here.
      Top Choice:
      Second Choice:
      Third Choice:

In telephone interviews, ranking should be limited to two or three alternatives at a time. In self-administered surveys and face-to-face interviews in which visual aids can be used, respondents should not be asked to rank more than five alternatives. If you insist on many alternatives, you can have respondents choose the top two or three and the bottom two or three.

Numerical Measures

Numerical measures ask respondents to produce numbers, as illustrated in Example 3.9.

EXAMPLE 3.9
Numerical Measures

1. How many of the following books and plays have you read?

    Oedipus Rex
    Pride and Prejudice
    The Vicar of Wakefield
    Bible
    Moby Dick
    The Glass Menagerie
    Number of books and plays I have read: _____

2. IF YOU HAVE READ THE *BIBLE:*
    How old were you when you first read the *Bible?*

    _____ years old

---

3. How important to a college graduate's education is each of the following books and plays? **Cross out** the one number that best describes your opinion of importance. The meaning of the numbers is as follows:

> 1 = Very important
> 8 = Neither important nor unimportant
> 15 = Very unimportant

Example

Hamlet   1   2   **X**   4   5   6   7   8   9   10   11   12   13   14   15

This person has assigned the reading of *Hamlet* a rating of 3.

Cross out ONE number

Oedipus Rex	1	2	3	4	5	6	7	8	9	10	11	12	13	14	15
Pride and Prejudice	1	2	3	4	5	6	7	8	9	10	11	12	13	14	15
The Vicar of Wakefield	1	2	3	4	5	6	7	8	9	10	11	12	13	14	15
Bible	1	2	3	4	5	6	7	8	9	10	11	12	13	14	15
Moby Dick	1	2	3	4	5	6	7	8	9	10	11	12	13	14	15
The Glass Menagerie	1	2	3	4	5	6	7	8	9	10	11	12	13	14	15

The first question asks respondents to record the number of books and plays they have read. The numbers produced by questions like this are called discrete. Other examples of discrete data are number of pregnancies, accidents, employees, patients, and so on. The second question asks for age. Age can start with zero and go up to the end of the human lifespan. The numbers produced by questions like this are called continuous. Other examples of continuous data are weight, height, years of survival, and scores on a test.

Sometimes, numerical data are classified as interval or ratio. With interval data, the distance between numbers or points have a real meaning. The most commonly quoted example is the Fahrenheit temperature scale. The 10-point difference between 70° and 80° is the same as the 10-point difference between 40° and 50°. Ratio measurements have a true zero, as in the Kelvin temperature scale. Fifty kelvins is half as warm as 100 kelvins. Because the Fahrenheit scale has an arbitrary zero, 40° is not half as hot as 80°. In practice, very few interval scales exist, and statistically, interval and ratio data tend to be treated the same. The term "numerical scales" or "measures" avoids confusion.

The third question in Example 3.9 asks the respondent to choose a number along a continuum. A similar way to obtain numerical data is through the use of rating scales that are presented along a printed line. In the following, respondents are asked to place an "X" on the line to describe the extent of their pain:

0____1____2____3____4____5____6____7____8____9____10

| | | Worst |
| No Pain | Moderate Pain | Possible Pain |

Scales like this lend themselves to reports like this: "At least 47% of respondents indicated that they had moderate pain (markings of 4, 5, or 6), whereas 10% had the worst possible pain (marking of 10)."

To aid in interpretation, decide on a length for the line, say, 10 centimeters or 10 inches. Then you can measure where along the line each respondent makes a mark and compute averages and other statistics. If one person places a mark at 1 inch (the low end of the scale), another at 1.3 inches, and a third at 3.3 inches, the average among the three respondents would be $1 + 1.3 + 3.3 = 5.6/3 = 1.866$.

4 Knowledge, Attitudes, and Behavior: Additional Tips When Creating Survey Questions

Although it is conventional in some fields, such as health, to think of measuring knowledge first and then attitudes and behavior, surveys tend to focus on attitudes.

Feelings and Intensity: Getting at the Attitude

An attitude is a general way of thinking, such as being liberal or conservative or being hostile or peaceable. The term "attitude" is often used to mean the same as opinion, belief, preference, feeling, and value. The following are typical of survey questions about attitudes:

- Do you favor gun control?
- Should the federal government do more to equalize income differences between the rich and the poor?
- How satisfied are you with your job?
- Which of the following are essential goals of a democratic society?
- Which description comes closest to defining the quality of your life?
- How healthy do you feel?
- Which is the best solution to illegal immigration?
- Do you favor an increase in taxes to support educational programs for very poor children?

Attitudes are very complex entities and difficult to define and measure. What are the characteristics that consistently and accurately distinguish liberals from conservatives? Does a universal definition of quality of life exist? Aspects of these questions are philosophical, but scientific and technical methods are available for producing attitude scales that are valid for specific survey needs. These methods are used by psychometricians to examine the statistical properties of questions to find out if they consistently and accurately distinguish people with the attitude from those without.

Attitudes are often contrasted with knowledge and behavior. How you feel about gun control laws, what you know about gun control laws, and what you personally do about guns may or may not be related logically.

Most survey experts agree that if you are interested in measuring concepts like political stance, religiosity, satisfaction (with job or quality of life or health) and you are not in a position to do a scientific experiment to validate the questions, you should use already existing and proven questions. These can be found through library searches of books and journals; by contacting college and university departments of medicine, public health, sociology, political science, and psychology; and by asking colleagues and associates to lend you their questions and measures. Books are available that contain attitudinal questions, but no central, updated clearinghouse exists. The fact is that finding attitude questions and scales is hard work. It can be costly in terms of the amount of time you have to spend to identify the right agency with the right questions. In some cases, payment is required. If you plan to use questions from existing surveys, check on who owns the copyright and whether you need the authors' permission to reproduce some or all questions.

Once you have identified one or more questions that meet the needs of your survey, check carefully to make certain that each is suitable for your survey's respondents. Is the language level appropriate? Does it truly ask what you need to know? You should have any borrowed questions reviewed and pretested.

A good way to pretest questions is to ask respondents to tell you in their own words what the question means to them. Tune in on the following dialogue with two potential survey respondents:

Surveyor: We are conducting a survey to find out if you are satisfied with your health care. Question one asks you to rate the importance of accessible care. The scale you will use has five response choices: definitely important, important, probably important, probably not important, and no opinion. Please tell me in your own words what this question means.

Respondent 1: You are asking me to tell you if I think getting an appointment with a doctor when I need one is important to me.

Respondent 2: To me, accessible care means not having to travel long distances and being able to park when you get there.

Surveyor: Based on what you have said, I see that the term "accessibility" is unclear at the present. The survey needs at least three questions to measure accessible care. The first will ask about the ease of getting an appointment, and the second and third will address time to travel and parking, respectively. I also plan to clearly define the response choices. For example, a response of a "very important" to a listed consideration would be one that must be addressed or you would choose to go elsewhere for care.

It often helps to think of attitude questions as having at least two components: how respondents feel and how strongly they feel (or believe). This is illustrated in Example 4.1.

EXAMPLE 4.1
Feelings and Intensity
in Attitude Questions

Edith Wilson, Eleanor Roosevelt, and Hillary Rodham Clinton, each of them the spouse of a U.S. president, have had considerable influence on U.S. policy. In general, do you approve of the role these spouses have played? Check **one** choice.

  [ ] Approve (**ask A**)
  [ ] Do not approve (**ask A**)
  [ ] Do not care/No opinion (**stop**)

How strongly do you feel about it? Check **one** choice.

  [ ] Very strongly
  [ ] Fairly strongly
  [ ] Not very strongly

Recall and Time: Getting at Behavior

Behavior refers to what respondents actually do. The following are examples of survey questions about respondents' behavior:

- Which of the following magazines and newspapers do you read at least once a month?
- How often do you exercise?
- Did you vote in the last election?
- How frequently do you go to church?
- In the past 3 years, how often did you apply for federal grants?

All questions about behavior are concerned with time, duration, or frequency. The preceding questions specify time periods: at least once a month, how frequently, the last election, and within the past 3 years.

Choose time periods that meet the survey's needs and that make sense to the respondent. You can obtain reliable information about events and activities that occurred years ago if they are important. People remember births, deaths, marriage, divorce, buying their first house, and so on. They also remember what they were doing at the time of great historical events like wars and assassinations and during natural disasters like fires, floods, and earthquakes. For most other events, do not expect people to remember past one year's time. You can, however, use yearly periods primarily for summary information:

- About how much money did you spend on vacations away from home in the past year?
- In the past 12 months, how often did you go for bicycle rides of 5 or more miles?

Asking respondents to give specific information over a long period of time leads to omissions:

Poor: In the past year, which of the following items of children's clothing did you buy from Outdoors Clothing Company?

Comment: Unless respondents have bought very few items of clothes for their children or buy exclusively from Outdoors Clothing Company, they might very easily forget.

Better: In the past 3 months, which of the following items of children's clothes did you buy from Outdoors Clothing Company?

Very short periods of time can adversely affect the accuracy or validity of an answer to a question about behavior:

Poor: In the past week, how often did you buy coffee, tea, bottled water, diet soda, or regular soda?

Comment: A question like this may produce invalid results because people may not have purchased any of the items during the past week. Nevertheless, because they do purchase and use them regularly, they may overreport by indicating a purchase in the past week that really occurred the week before.

Better: In the past 3 weeks, how often did you buy coffee, tea, bottled water, diet soda, or regular soda?

Because questions about behavior have a time element, you are dependent on respondents' ability to recall. To jog the memory, use lists, as illustrated in Example 4.2.

EXAMPLE 4.2
Using a List to Help Respondents Remember Their Actions

This question is about your leisure activities. Since last January, did you do any of these activities? Check **yes** or **no** for each.

	Yes (1)	No (2)
Go to a movie	1	2
Eat out for pleasure	1	2
Window shop	1	2
Go to the theater	1	2

$\rightarrow$

	Yes (1)	No (2)
Read for pleasure	1	2
Go for a run	1	2
Go for a hike	1	2
Ride a bicycle	1	2
Go fishing	1	2
Do gardening	1	2

The advantage of a list is its capacity for reminding respondents of events they may have forgotten. To be maximally helpful, the list should be inclusive. An inclusive list can go on for many pages, which is confusing and boring. One way to get around the long-list problem is to divide a question into its component parts, as illustrated in Example 4.3.

EXAMPLE 4.3
Dividing the Question:
How to Avoid Long Lists and
Still Get the Behaviors You Need

1. Since last January, have you participated in any of the following activities? Answer **yes** or **no** for each.

Shopping for pleasure	1	2	If yes, answer Question 3
Religious groups	1	2	If yes, answer Question 5

2. Since last January, did you play any of the following sports? Answer **yes** or **no** for each sport.

	Yes (1)	No (2)
Basketball	1	2
Baseball	1	2
Football	1	2
Bowling	1	2
Other—please name:	1	2
Other—please name:	1	2

By presenting a list to respondents, you may encourage them to use only the categories in the survey, and this may result in a loss of information. To avoid losing information, you can add an "other" category as is done in Question 2 in Example 4.3. By adding this option, you are including an open question and must be prepared to interpret and catalogue the answers.

EXERCISE

Will the questions in Examples 4.2 and 4.3 produce categorical, ordinal, or numerical data?

■ ANSWER ■

Categorical

Regulating Difficulty and Threat:
Getting at Knowledge

Knowledge questions are included in surveys to achieve the following objectives:

- Determine if people have enough knowledge about a topic to warrant asking their opinion about it
- Identify gaps in knowledge that warrant education, advertising, or publicity or other kinds of information campaigns
- Help explain attitudes and behavior

Example 4.4 illustrates the three main uses of knowledge questions.

EXAMPLE 4.4
Using Knowledge Questions in Surveys

The University Medical Center is concerned that women are not routinely getting Pap smears. These screening tests are essential for early diagnosis of cervical cancer. A survey is taken of all women who come for gynecological services in a one-year period.

1. *Knowledge of a Topic.* A primary survey purpose is to find out what women know. Accordingly, questions are asked about knowledge of the purpose of Pap smears, how they are performed, and how frequently they should be obtained.

2. *Educational Needs.* The answers to the questions are used to find out if an educational campaign is needed and, if so, what topics should be included. The survey's results reveal that nearly 60% of the women do not correctly answer the question about the purpose of the test. Only 20% know how often to have a Pap smear, using guidelines set by the American Cancer

Society or the American College of Obstetricians and Gynecologists (the two groups differ). Nearly 92% of women who say they had at least one Pap smear know how it is performed. Based on these findings, the surveyors recommend the preparation of educational brochures in English, Spanish, and Portuguese, the main languages spoken by patients. The survey team also recommends a media campaign to encourage women to seek Pap smears.

3. *Explaining Attitudes and Behavior.* One survey question asks about the convenience of clinic hours. The survey team compares the women who say they favor increased clinic hours for screening tests with those who do not. The team's analysis demonstrates that women who correctly answered the questions about the purpose of Pap tests are definitely more favorably disposed (margin of 10 to 1) toward increased hours of clinic operation.

The boundary between attitude and knowledge questions is sometimes blurred. Consider these questions:

1. Using your best guess, what percentage of people do not report some of their pay to the Internal Revenue Service?

2. In your view, what is the best way to prevent influenza in people over 75 years of age?

Are the above questions asking for attitudes or knowledge? The first question looks like a knowledge question because it asks for a fact or a percentage. Estimates do exist of the proportion of people earning money and not declaring it to the IRS, but because most of us probably do not know the percentage, we guess. For many, the guess is as much a reflection of how much cheating we think is going on as an attempt to come up with an accurate estimate.

The second question seems like an attitude question. In fact, it is a knowledge question because a correct answer is available: Give them flu shots.

Knowledge questions are sometimes disguised so as to reduce their threatening appearance. This is done with phrases like "in your opinion," "using your best guess," and "have you heard or have you read that . . . ?"

Knowledge questions can vary in their difficulty. The easiest questions are relatively general and ask for recall of current or significant information. The most difficult questions ask the respondent to recall, understand, interpret, and apply information in innovative ways. Consider this example:

> *Easier:* Have you heard or read about President Kennedy's assassination?
>
> *More difficult:* From this list, select the name of President Kennedy's probable assassin.
>
> *Even more difficult:* Five cities are circled on this map. Please show me the location of the city in which President Kennedy was assassinated.

The first question is the easiest because the significance of the assassination suggests that nearly everyone (not just Americans) will have heard or read about the assassination. The second question requires recall of a name. President Kennedy was assassinated in 1963, and for many, the assassin's name has faded from memory. Others may have never learned the name. The use of a list helps respondents remember. The third question requires knowledge of the name of the city and its location on a map, and because it involves recall and understanding of geography, it is the hardest of the three questions.

Most surveys of knowledge are not achievement tests in the classical sense. They are not used to grade or promote students or find out what they have learned. You may be more interested in finding out how many respondents do not know about something. Many surveys of knowledge include "do not know" or "no opinion" response choices. These choices also help remove some of the threat associated with knowledge questions. Suppose you were surveying respondents about the physical environment. You might ask a question like the following:

A fossil of an ocean fish was found in a rock outcrop on a mountain. Which of the following best describes the meaning of this finding? Select **one** choice only.

Fish once lived on the mountain.

The relative humidity was once very high.

The mountain was raised up after the fish died.

Fish used to be amphibians like toads and frogs.

The fossil fish was probably carried to the mountain by a great flood.

I don't know.

By providing an "I don't know" category, people who might otherwise just guess are given a place to put their response. But beware! "I don't know" is sometimes used by those who are too lazy or do not want to think about the question even when doing so could result in the correct answer.

Demographics: Who Are the Respondents?

Demographic information consists of facts about a respondent's age, race/ethnicity, education job, gender, whether married or not, geographic place of residence, type of residence, size of family, and so on.

Compare the two typical demographic questions about race
and ethnicity in Example 4.5.

EXAMPLE 4.5
Two Questions About Race and Ethnicity

Question 1

4. Race

Fill ONE circle for the race that you consider
youself to be.

      o White
      o Black or Negro
      o Indian (Amer.) (Print the name
          of the enrolled or principal tribe) ↓

If Indian (Amer.), print the name of the
enrolled or principal tribe._____ →
[_]

      o Eskimo
      o Aleut

<u>Asian or Pacific Islander (API)</u>

o Chinese	o Japanese
o Filipino ■	o Asian Indian
o Hawaiian	o Samoan
o Korean	o Guamanian
o Vietnamese	o Other API ↓

If Other Asian or Pacific Islander (API),
print one group: for example, Hmong,
Fijian, Laotian, Thai, Tongan, Pakistani,
Cambodian, and so on. _____ →
[_ _ _ _ _ _ _ _ _ _ _ _ _ _ _ _ _ _]

If Other race, print race _____ →

      o Other race (Print race) ↑

Question 2

What is your race/ethnicity? Check **one** only.

[ ] White, non-Latino
[ ] White, Latino (or Hispanic)
[ ] Black, African American
[ ] Asian: Chinese, Japanese
[ ] Southeast Asian: Vietnamese, Cambodian, Hmong, Laotian, Chinese Vietnamese
[ ] Other Asian (not Chinese, Japanese, or Southeast Asian)
[ ] Pacific Islanders (Samoan, Filipino, etc.)
[ ] Native American (American Indian)
[ ] Other (specify) _____

The aim of the two questions in Example 4.5 is to collect a vital statistic: the race or ethnicity of the respondents. The two questions differ in the following ways:

- Question 1 gives the choice of Black or Negro. Question 2 gives an open choice: Black, African American.

- Question 1 refers to American Indians and asks for the name of the enrolled or principal tribe. Question 2 gives the choice of Native American (American Indian) and does not ask for the name of the respondent's tribe.

- Question 1 includes as choices Hawaiian, Korean, Asian Indian, Guamanian, Eskimo, and Aleut. Question 2 does not mention these but does include Chinese Vietnamese.

Questions 1 and 2 differ because they were posed for surveys with entirely distinct purposes and groups of respondents. Question 1 comes from the U.S. Bureau of the Census official

1990 Census form. The question was asked of everyone in the United States in 1989. Question 2 comes from a 1991 survey of low-income women who participated in a federally funded project in California to improve maternal and infant outcomes through prenatal care.

Surveys differ in purpose and in target respondents. Before asking for demographic information, learn about the likely characteristics of the target group. Question 1 is concerned with the racial/ethnic characteristics of everyone in the United States. Question 2 addresses only low-income women in one state. If the Census Bureau had asked Question 2, many races would have been lumped into "other," necessitating a great deal of work to unscramble categories. If the prenatal study had asked Question 1, many categories might have remained un-checked; the study would not have obtained data on the number of respondents who were Chinese Vietnamese, a group that was important in the study of prenatal care.

Another difference between Questions 1 and 2 is use of language. In its 1990 census, the Census Bureau used the classification "Negro." By 1991, this term was no longer favored; it was therefore excluded from Question 2 and "Afri-can American" was used. At about the same time, "Native American" began to coexist with and even supplant "American Indian" as a category, and Question 2's response choices also reflect this.

Question 2 offers as one of the choices White, Latino (or Hispanic), but Question 1 does not include this choice. This group of people constitutes a large segment of the U.S. popu-lation. Strictly speaking, at least in 1990, Latinos were not considered a racial or ethnic group. The Census Bureau asked about Spanish *origin*, and the prenatal care study asked about country of birth, as shown in Example 4.6.

EXAMPLE 4.6
Asking About Origin or Country of Birth

1. Asked by the Bureau of the Census:

---

7. Is this person of Spanish/Hispanic origin?

Fill ONE circle for each person.

o No (not Spanish/Hispanic)
o Yes, Mexican, Mexican-Am., Chicano
o Yes, Puerto Rican ■
o Yes, Cuban
o Yes, other Spanish/Hispanic
(Print one group, for example:
Argentinean, Colombian,
Dominican, Nicaraguan, Salvadoran,
Spaniard, and so on.) ↓

If **Yes, other Spanish/Hispanic,**
print one group ——————→

---

2. Asked in a survey of low-income women receiving prenatal care in California:

If you are White, Latina (or Hispanic), then what is the
country of your birth? Check **one** only.

[ ] United States
[ ] Mexico
[ ] Central America
[ ] Caribbean
[ ] South America
[ ] Spain or Portugal
[ ] Other: _____

An important distinction between the two questions is in the specificity of the responses. The Census Bureau's question provides data on the precise country of birth in South and Central America. The California question asks for less detailed information about these continents but singles out Mexico because of the large number of people of Mexican origin in the state. The two questions also differ in their use of Latino, a term commonly used in California by 1990.

Why do surveyors ask respondents demographic questions? A major reason is to tell who the respondents are. How old are they? Where do they live? What is their race/ethnicity? Demographic data are also useful in helping explain the results of surveys. In a survey of child-rearing practices, you might ask questions like these: Do differences exist among younger and older respondents? Among respondents from differing parts of the country? From differing countries of origin?

Demographic data are also needed to help explore the findings of research and of other surveys. Consider the survey team's task in Example 4.7.

EXAMPLE 4.7
Exploring With Demographics

The community is concerned that many people are not taking advantage of preventive health services like immunizations for children, influenza vaccinations for the elderly, prenatal care, and yearly mammograms for women over 50 years of age. A number of surveys are planned to help explore the barriers that deter people from using these services.

A team has designed the first survey to find out about barriers to the use of prenatal care. Their review of the published research reveals that currently unmarried women begin their care late and do not stay with it continuously. The also have poor birth outcomes. When compared to the babies of married women, the babies of unmarried mothers are more frequently of low weight and premature. The survey team is interested in exploring factors other than (or together with) marital status that may help explain inappropriate use of prenatal care.

The survey team reasons that currently unmarried women may be younger than other women. Births to very young mothers are riskier than other births, so age may be a contributing factor to the poor outcomes. The team also suggests that unmarried women may also be poorer than others, and that being poor is often associated with lack of access to and use of health services. They also consider that education may be a factor in the use of health services. If they find that the women in the community who are currently unmarried are also relatively young, then the surveyors will be especially interested in finding out about the extent of their completed education. Accordingly, the survey team includes demographic questions on women's birth date, income, and education.

Age, Income, and Education

To learn about age, ask for the precise date of birth. If you ask for age, some people will tell you their age that day, and others will tell you their age on their next birthday which happens to be next week. In a survey that takes, say, 6 months to complete, even the most accurate statements of age are difficult to interpret. Suppose you ask Respondent A his age today, Respondent B her age 2 weeks from today, and Respondent C his age 6 months from today. One year from today, you begin to summarize the data. Do you compute the ages on the basis of where the respondents were 12 months ago? Do you make any allowances for the fact that by the time you got around to Respondent C, Respondents A and B had aged? If you have the exact date of birth, you can much more easily compute exact frequencies and averages. You can pick one date, say, 6 months after the start of a 1-year survey, and compute everyone's exact age on that date.

Income questions are often considered "sensitive." In the United States, income is considered a private, even personal matter. Asking for income in surveys requires special handling. One way of protecting the respondent's privacy and yet giving you the data you need is to ask for income in terms of categories, such as between $40,000 and $50,000 or between $50,001 and $60,000. Remember to provide mutually exclusive categories:

Poor: Which best describes your personal income in 1994? Check **one** only.

> [ ] $35,000 or less
> [ ] $35,000 to $55,000
> [ ] $55,000 to $75,000
> [ ] $75,000 or more

Comment: The categories overlap so that a person whose income was $35,000 could correctly choose A or B. The categories for $55,000 and $75,000 overlap as well.

Better: Which best describes your personal income in 1994? Check **one** only.

> [ ] $35,000 or less
> [ ] $35,001 to $55,000
> [ ] $55,001 to $75,000
> [ ] $75,001 or more

When asking income questions with categorical choices, make sure the categories are meaningful. Wealthier people should be given many choices above the median income for the community, whereas poorer people should be given many choices below the median, as illustrated in Example 4.8.

EXAMPLE 4.8
Asking Questions About
Incomes in Two Settings

Setting 1

A survey is being conducted of all people who used Travelmore Travel Agency for three or more trips out of the country that lasted at least 2 weeks. One question asks about household income:

Which of the following best describes *your* income this
  current year? Check **one** only.

        [ ] $50,000 or less
        [ ] $50,001 to $100,000
        [ ] $100,001 to $200,000
        [ ] $200,001 or more

Setting 2

A survey is being conducted to find out where low-income families obtain mental health services. People are approached outside schools, churches, and supermarkets. One question asks about income:

Which of the following best describes *your* income this
  current year? Check **one** only.

        [ ] $10,000 or less
        [ ] $10,001 to $20,000
        [ ] $20,001 to $30,000
        [ ] $30,001 or more

Whenever possible, ask for precise information about income. The Census Bureau asks for total income. The respondent is asked to specify and add income from wages, salaries, commissions and tips; self-employment income from farms and other businesses; interest, dividends, rental income, incomes from estates and trusts; royalties, social security, or railroad retirement pay; Supplemental Security Income, Aid to Families with Dependent Children, or other public assistance or welfare; retirement, survivor, or disability pensions; and child support, unemployment benefits, and alimony.

When asking questions about income, you must specify a time period. Do you want to know about average income over 3 years? total income over the past year? You must also decide if you want a particular person's income or the household's. If you want the household income, you must define household as it pertains to income. An infant may be in the household but is not likely to be contributing income to it. Two or more unrelated adults may constitute a household if they contribute to some predefined proportion of the household's income.

Questions about education should be selected to meet the needs of the survey. A survey of physicians' education will have different choices from those given to a broader group of respondents, as illustrated in Example 4.9.

EXAMPLE 4.9
Two Questions About Education

Question 1

A survey of physicians in an academic medical center is interested in finding out how many of them have obtained academic degrees. The survey asks this question:

Do you have any of the following degrees? Circle yes **or** no for each degree listed.

	Yes (1)	No (2)
Master's degree in public health	1	2
Master's degree in business administration	1	2
PhD (specify field: _____)	1	2
Doctor of Dental Surgery	1	2
Juris Doctor	1	2
Doctor of Veterinary Medicine	1	2
Other (specify: _____)	1	2
Other (specify: _____)	1	2

Question 2

A survey of customers at Travelmore Travel Agency asks this question about their education:

How much school have you completed? Check **one** for the highest level completed or degree received. If currently enrolled in school, check the level of previous grade attended or highest degree received.

[ ] 12th grade or less
[ ] High school graduate or equivalent
[ ] Some college but no degree
[ ] Associate degree (academic or occupational)
[ ] Bachelor's degree
[ ] Master's degree
[ ] Professional school degree (such as MD, LLB, JD, DDS, DVM)
[ ] Doctorate (such as PhD, EdD, DrPH)

In a survey of teens' education, specify most categories before 12th grade (such as 9th grade, 8th grade, 7th grade, 6th grade, or lower); you may wish to include "Other" as a category. The following are guidelines for asking questions to get demographic information.

Guidelines for Asking Questions on Vital Statistics and Demographics

- *Learn the characteristics of the survey's targeted respondents.* You do this so that the response categories make sense. You can find out about respondents by checking census data, interviewing the respondents, asking others who know about the respondents, and reviewing recent literature.

- *Decide on appropriate level of specificity.* An appropriate level is one that will meet the needs of the survey but not be too cumbersome for the respondent. Remember, a self-administered survey and telephone interview should have no more than four or five response categories. An interviewer should use visual aids if more than five categories are used.

- *Ask for exact information in an open-ended format.* One way to avoid having many response categories is to ask the respondents to tell you in their own words the answers to demographic questions. Respondents can give their date of birth, age as of a specified date, income, ZIP code, area code, and so on.

- *Use current words and terms.* The words used to describe people's backgrounds change over time. Outmoded words are sometimes offensive. The world's geography changes, and people's affiliations and commitments alter. If you borrow questions from other sources, check to see that they use words in a contemporary way. Terms like "household" and definitions of concepts like wealth and poverty also change over time.

■ *Decide if you want comparability.* If you want to compare one group of respondents with another, consider borrowing questions and response choices from other surveys. For example, if you want to compare the education of people in your survey with the typical American's in 1990, then use the question that was asked in the census. If you borrow questions, check to see that the words and terms are still relevant and that the response choices are meaningful.

Exercises

EXERCISE 1: Read the description of the survey plan and then follow the directions given below it.

Description of Survey Plan

The Outdoors Mail Order Company is planning a mail survey of 150 customers who purchased goods within the past months. A Spanish-language version of the survey will be available upon request. The purpose of the survey is to find out to what extent a market exists for household and kitchen goods with an "outdoors" flavor. For example, many of the fabrics used by the company on furniture and for tablecloths and other linens have patterns of lakes, forests, and mountains. Pots and pans are fashioned after those used on camping trips.

The survey is expected to take no more than 10 minutes and will only use closed-ended questions. All responses will be confidential.

91

The survey has been designed to answer these questions:

1. How old is the average customer?
2. What proportion of customers live in differing geographic regions of the United States?
3. How many people are willing to purchase each of a selected list of household and kitchen goods sold by the company?
4. On average, how many purchases did customers make in the past 6 months?
5. How satisfied were customers with the service? with the quality of the products?
6. Are differences found in numbers and types of purchases that can be accounted for by age and satisfaction?

The following is an outline of the survey.

Outline for Survey of Market for Household and Kitchen Goods

Topic	Number of Questions	Information Collected
Age	1	Date of birth
Region of the country	1	Northeast, Middle Atlantic, Southeast, Midwest, Northwest, Southwest, West
Kitchen goods	5	Type of kitchen goods would purchase, if any (e.g., furniture, dishes, linens)
Household goods	5	Type of household goods would purchase, if any (e.g., furniture, pictures)
Frequency of past purchases from Outdoors	1	If ever, once before, twice, three or more times
Satisfaction	2	Satisfied with service, with purchase: extremely satisfied to extremely dissatisfied

Directions

Answer these questions using the description of the survey and the outline.

1. Describe the context in which the survey will take place by describing its purpose, respondents, surveyors, responses, timing, resources, and privacy requirements.

2. Write the questions for the survey using the above outline as your guide. (Do not worry about introducing the survey, the order the questions should take, or any special graphic requirements.)

3. For each question in the survey, tell whether you will be obtaining categorical, ordinal, or numerical data.

EXERCISE 2: Write a survey that answers these questions:

1. Does this book achieve each of its stated objectives?

2. On the whole, how helpful were the book's examples in assisting readers to learn?

3. How practical are each of this book's guidelines and checklists?

4. Do readers usually enjoy reading the text and doing the exercises?

5. Do readers who do and do not recommend this book to others have similar school- or job-related responsibilities?

6. Does a difference exist in younger and older readers in terms of their perceptions of the book's helpfulness and practicality?

ANSWERS

EXERCISE 1

1. The Survey's Context

Purpose. The purpose of the survey is to find out if a market exists for kitchen and household goods that are sold by Outdoors and, if so, to characterize it. The characteristics of concern are age, region of the country, willingness to purchase selected kitchen and household goods, frequency of purchases, and satisfaction with purchases and service.

Respondents. The respondents are 150 customers who ordered from the company within the past 6 months.

Surveyor. The mail survey

Responses. A variety of responses can be expected including ratings of satisfaction and categories to describe where people live geographically.

Timing. The survey is to take 10 minutes of each respondent's time.

Resources. A Spanish translation is needed

Privacy. The responses are to be confidential.

2. Questions for the Survey

What is your date of birth?

[ ] [ ] 19 [ ]
Month Day   Year

In which region of the country do you live? Check **one** answer only.

        [ ] Northeast
        [ ] Middle Atlantic
        [ ] Southeast
        [ ] Midwest
        [ ] Northwest
        [ ] Southwest
        [ ] West

Check yes **or** no to indicate whether you would purchase each of the following if it had an outdoors theme. By outdoors theme, we mean fabrics that depict lakes, rivers, mountains, and so on and styles that are based on camping, fishing, and hiking gear.

Would you buy each of these kitchen goods if they were similar in appearance to those used when camping, fishing, or hiking and/or if they had an outdoors theme or design?

	Yes (1)	No (2)	Don't Know/ No Opinion (3)
Pots and pans	1	2	3
Flatware (knives, forks, spoons)	1	2	3
Dishes and glasses	1	2	3
Table linens (napkins, placemats, tablecloths)	1	2	3
Floor coverings	1	2	3

Would you buy each of these household goods if they were similar in appearance to those used when camping, fishing, or hiking and/or had an outdoors theme or design?

	Yes (1)	No (2)	Don't Know/ No Opinion (3)
Furniture for the living room	1	2	3
Floor coverings	1	2	3
Pictures and photographs	1	2	3
Bedroom furniture	1	2	3
Furniture for a study or den	1	2	3

In the past 6 months, how many items did you purchase from Outdoors? Select **one** best answer.

[ ] 1
[ ] 2 to 4
[ ] 5 to 10
[ ] More than 10

How satisfied are you with Outdoors' service and quality? Circle **one**.

	Extremely Satisfied (4)	Satisfied (3)	Dissatisfied (2)	Extremely Dissatisfied (1)	No Opinion (0)
Service	4	3	2	1	0
Quality	4	3	2	1	0

3. Types of Data Obtained From Each Question

Date of birth:	numerical
Region of the country:	categorical
Willingness to purchase kitchen goods:	categorical
Willingness to purchase household goods:	categorical
Frequency of purchases:	numerical
Satisfaction with service and quality:	ordinal

EXERCISE 2

1. Does this book achieve each of the following objectives? Answer yes **or** no for each objective.

Objectives for the Reader	Yes (1)	No (2)	Uncertain/ Don't Know (0)
Understand a survey's context (e.g., cultural, economic, political)	1	2	0
Ask valid survey questions	1	2	0
Compare the characteristics of open and closed questions	1	2	0
Distinguish between response formats that use categorical, ordinal, and numerical measurement	1	2	0
Identify questions that are written correctly	1	2	0
Apply techniques for asking questions to learn about behavior	1	2	0
Apply techniques for asking questions to learn about attitudes	1	2	0
Apply techniques for asking questions to learn about knowledge	1	2	0
Apply techniques for asking questions to learn about demographics	1	2	0

2. On the whole, did the book's examples assist you in learning? Please circle **one.**

Definitely yes	1
Probably yes	2
Probably no	3
Definitely no	4
Uncertain/no opinion	5

3. How practical are each of the following guidelines and checklists for asking survey questions? Please rate the practicality of **each** guideline and checklist using this scale:

   1 = Very impractical

   2 = Impractical

   3 = Practical

   4 = Very practical

   0 = Uncertain/no opinion

*Please make **one** rating for each
of the listed guidelines and checklists.*

Guidelines					
Guidelines for Asking Survey Questions	1	2	3	4	0
Guidelines for Using Conventional Language When Asking Survey Questions	1	2	3	4	0
Guidelines for Asking Closed Questions With Ordered Responses	1	2	3	4	0
Guidelines for Asking Questions on Vital Statistics and Demographics	1	2	3	4	0
Checklists					
Checklist for Deciding the Survey's Context	1	2	3	4	0
Checklist for Deciding Between Open and Closed Questions	1	2	3	4	0

4. Did you usually enjoy reading the text and doing the exercises? Please rate each.

	Almost Never (1)	Rarely (2)	Sometimes (3)	Frequently (4)	Almost Always (5)
Reading the text	1	2	3	4	5
Doing the exercises	1	2	3	4	5

5. Do you recommend this book to others who have similar responsibilities for asking survey questions? Please circle **one**.

Definitely yes	1
Probably yes	2
Definitely no	3
Probably no	4
Uncertain/no opinion	0

6. For which purposes do you plan to write survey questions? Check all that apply.

[ ] Evaluation/research

[ ] Policy

[ ] Program planning or development

[ ] Needs assessment/marketing

[ ] Other: _____

_____

_____

_____

7. In which settings do you plan to or are you actually asking survey questions? Check all that apply.

    [   ] School, college, or university
    [   ] Government
    [   ] Business
    [   ] Health professions
    [   ] Law
    [   ] Other: _____

    _____

    _____

    _____

8. What is your date of birth? Write 01 for January, 02 for February, and so on. Write 01 for the first day of the month, 02 for the second, and so on.

        [__ __] Month   [__ __] Date   [19 __ __] Year

Suggested Readings

Babbie, E. (1990). *Survey research methods*. Belmont, CA: Wadsworth.

A fundamental reference on how to conduct survey research. Good examples of survey questions with accompanying rules for asking questions.

Bradburn, N. M., & Sudman, S. (1992). The current status of questionnaire design. In P. N. Biemer, R. M. Groves, L. E. Lyberg, N. A. Mathiowetz, & S. Sudman (Eds.), *Measurement errors in surveys*. New York: John Wiley.

Addresses many of the major issues in designing questionnaires and asking questions.

Converse, J. (1987). *Survey research in the United States*. Berkeley: University of California Press.

An overview and good examples of the how surveys are used in the United States; helpful in understanding the context of survey research.

101

Fink, A. (1993). *Evaluation fundamentals: Guiding health programs, research and policy*. Newbury Park, CA: Sage.

Gives rules for asking questions and responses; provides a checklist for creating or adapting measures; and discusses the roles of categorical, ordinal, and numerical data in measurement and data analysis.

Fink, A., & Kosecoff, J. (1985). *How to conduct surveys: A step by step guide*. Beverly Hills, CA: Sage.

Gives many examples of survey questions and contains rules and guidelines for asking questions.

Fowler, F. J. (1993). *Survey research methods*. Newbury Park, CA: Sage.

Chapter 6 deals with designing and evaluating survey questions, including defining objectives.

Fowler, F. J., & Mangione, T. W. (1990). *Standardized survey interviewing: Minimizing interviewer related error*. Newbury Park, CA: Sage.

Contains good survey question examples and tells how to minimize error by standardizing the surveyor and the questionnaire.

Frey, J. H. (1989). *Survey research by telephone*. Newbury Park, CA: Sage.

Gives excellent examples of questions and how to get the information you need from telephone surveys.

Kosecoff, J., & Fink, A. (1982). *Evaluation basics: A practitioner's manual*. Beverly Hills, CA: Sage.

Tells how to write questions and how to use them appropriately in open and closed formats.

Lavrakas, P. J. (1987). *Telephone survey methods: Sampling, selection, and supervision.* Newbury Park, CA: Sage.

Discusses questions in the context of telephone surveys.

McDowell, I., & Newell, C. (1987). *Measuring health: A guide to rating scales.* New York: Oxford University Press.

Contains a very good compendium of scales to use in asking questions pertaining to health.

Miller, D. C. (1991). *Handbook of research design and social measurement.* Newbury Park, CA: Sage.

Discusses and defines all possible components of social research. Part 6 has selected sociometric scales and indexes and is a very good source of questions pertaining to social status, group structure, organizational structure, job satisfaction, community, family and marriage, and attitudes.

Schuman, H., & Presser, S. (1981). *Question and answers in attitude surveys.* New York: Academic Press.

Raises and addresses many of the important issues in designing questions about attitudes; contains good examples.

Stewart, A. L., & Ware, J. E. (1992). *Measuring functioning and well-being: The medical outcomes study approach.* Durham, NC: Duke University Press.

Tells of the design and validation of a wide range of self-reported functioning and well-being measures developed for a large U.S. study of health care; very good source of questions.

Sudman, S., & Bradburn, N. M. (1982). *Asking questions.* San Francisco: Jossey-Bass.

Very good source for examples of how to write questions pertaining to attitudes, knowledge, behavior, and demographics.

About the Author

ARLENE FINK, PhD, is Professor of Medicine and Public Health at the University of California, Los Angeles. She is on the Policy Advisory Board of UCLA's Robert Wood Johnson Clinical Scholars Program, a health research scientist at the Veterans Administration Medical Center in Sepulveda, California, and president of Arlene Fink Associates. She has conducted evaluations throughout the United States and abroad and has trained thousands of health professionals, social scientists, and educators in program evaluation. Her published works include nearly 100 monographs and articles on evaluation methods and research. She is coauthor of *How to Conduct Surveys* and author of *Evaluation Fundamentals: Guiding Health Programs, Research, and Policy* and *Evaluation for Education and Psychology.*